# Know Yourself

## Spiritual Profiling of the Four Distinct Personalities of Mankind

ALEXANDER O. EMOGHENE

Copyright © 2021 Alexander O. Emoghene.

All rights reserved. No part of this book may be reproduced, stored, or transmitted by any means—whether auditory, graphic, mechanical, or electronic—without written permission of both publisher and author, except in the case of brief excerpts used in critical articles and reviews. Unauthorized reproduction of any part of this work is illegal and is punishable by law.

# CONTENTS



## PART 1

# PART 2

# A NOTE TO THE READER

To clarify the differences between each personality, God made man balanced in spirit, soul, and body, then imbued mankind with supernatural abilities to carry out His dominion on Earth (Genesis 1:26–27).

My hope and prayer for this book is to reinforce the restoration process of man through Christ and to facilitate the revelation of God in bringing mankind back to his original purpose. It will take a strong combination of both leader and follower personalities to bring mankind to the place of total authority and deliverance to emerge as the ideal human.

From the kingdom perspective, social scientists and the evolutionists, all will find the various concepts in this book vital for judging how best to determine the growth of learning. In addition, the strategies conveyed in this book, will further encourage the applicability to the improvement of structural learning at levels in different disciplines across societies at large. The scriptures paint the original picture, illustrating these unique personalities in clear terms.

In secular study structures, people are directed to see themselves as possessing just one of these personalities, whereas from the kingdom standpoint, everyone possesses all these personalities. The process of restoration, however, will reveal to the individual which personality is primary, and the ones which are secondary, thus bringing balance to the person's heart.

On a massive scale, when a society is armed with such understanding, they can readily accept and make provisions to mine the vast wealth of gifts and talent buried within the general population.

Diversity in the larger communities is a treasure to any society. If that strength can be harnessed through strategic planning, teaching, and the creation of opportunities in the education system, students grow to know their personality and the importance of exploring and using their "power," as it were. This structure will provide a platform formidable enough to facilitate the discovery and introduction of new, meaningful, and impactful transformational leadership.

As you read further, you will discover the rich reserve that God has placed in you and how you can tap into it. My hope is that you will appreciate yourself, your peers, and possibly find your calling and assignment in God. After your discovery, you will also be able to weaponize these discoveries to create positive impact among your families, your communities, and your nation.

What I hope and pray is that this book will fulfill its purpose, which is to bring you to a true place of healing and empowerment through self-discovery, gift-recovery, and God-discovery. A place where we realize that all these qualities are buried deep inside us by God as potential to be explored, recovered, and enjoyed (Psalm 23:3).

Happy reading!

# ACKNOWLEDGMENTS

First and Foremost, to His most excellency, the supreme creator of all things, the omniscient, the Father of glory and the wonder of the ages to come, The Lord Jesus Christ, His manifested presence in the flesh and the bringer of God's presence and his excellence, the Holy Spirit, I Thank You for enabling me to write this book.

I also want to appreciate my sweetheart and darling wife, Judith for being that relentless voice of encouragement to me, from the moment I put pen to paper, to the completion of this book. Thank you for all your support and always being by my side, you make it all easy to fulfil God's will.

Last but not least, I would like to appreciate the faithful leadership and members on the board of our church, Claypot Church International; pastors, Cosmea Kambel and Tamara Bronner, your consistency and constant availability to step in and fulfil God's work does not go unnoticed. Also, to Pastor Carl Dennis, Pastor of Kingdom Central Birmingham, and my dean at KISOM (Kingsway international school of ministries) for your invaluable advice and support in this process. Also, to the members and the family of Claypot Church International, I express my gratitude for your prayers, support, loyalty and submission which allowed me to develop the concepts in this book.

I am most grateful to all the above and all others I have not mentioned, that contributed directly or indirectly to the fulfilment of this book, bless you all.

# ENDORSEMENT

The model of discipleship in the 21ˢᵗ Century church is re-ceiving an upgrade from some of the religious patterns of the past. Several years ago at a state prophetic summit, I proph-esied that the Lord was going to shift the discipleship model of the church from a shepherd sheep to the embracing of the four-faced feature that we find in Ezekiel. As I read Ps Alexander Emoghenes book draft I felt like I was reading the operation manual for how this discipleship is to be outworked. I highly endorse not only the apostolic revelation write in this book to you but also the minister who has written it. Ps Alexander is a dynamic minister in the body of Christ and a great equipped of the saints. I encourage you to work through the chapters slowly and prayerfully asking the Holy Spirit to transform your thinking and perceptions about who you are and what you are capable of.

David Balestri
Convenor of the Australian coalition
of apostolic leaders (ACAL)

"Know Yourself" is a prerequisite for maximizing your God-given potential and minimizing liabilities in one's life. Self-discovering is an art and a skill to be developed at all costs if destiny must be fulfilled.

In his newest book, "Know Yourself" Pastor Alexander has captured the essence and importance of knowing oneself as it plays a pivotal role in man's ultimate fulfillment of his God-ordained destiny.

The book "Know Yourself" is a compendium of time-tested concepts, a concise book that illuminates and helps us to understand, clarifying the differences of mankind's personalities. In the end, that man will discover, develop and deploy their innate capacities as they seek to fulfill their God-ordained destinies on the earth. In straightforward terms, Pastor Emoghene catalogs the benefits and critical factors that must be engaged in knowing yourself that engenders the corporate man to live out his/her full potential.

We have seen destinies truncated and destroyed whether in families, ministries, or any enterprise because of the ignorance of self. Consequently, man is unfulfilled in life and frustrated at unprecedented levels with the dream of living a fulfilled life a figment of their imagination. The book "Know Yourself" surfaced for such a time as this and to help empower the Church and re-establish God's principles on a self-discovering as articulated in His Word.

In this book, Pastor Alexander Emoghene is used by God as a prophetic voice and a catalyst to give the Church a mentality makeover and enable the average believer to understand what I call human authenticity thus adequately maximizing potential to becoming all that God has ordained.

I prayerfully recommend this book to you, your family, and your ministries. It will enhance your understanding of and confidence in knowing who you are.

Dr. Richard ONEBAMOI
Living Stone World Worship Centre
Brussels, Belgium

"Know Yourself" has awakened in me a new form of curiosity; I was not aware of the 4 personalities we have as human beings. To me this book is a guide to the exploration of my true self and the 4 personalities in me. Besides that, it's a very enjoyable read. Alexander has written this book in a way that creates interest and builds up one's curiosity such that you would want to read it in one go; continuously wanting to know what is coming next, what will I be learning next?

This book should be considered a textbook for Christians. like Jews have the Talmud, we should have more teachings like this to dig into the infinite wisdom of the Holy Bible, and to acquire more wisdom and understanding. This is a must read for every Christian in search of his of her purpose in life. This book will help you in your expedition to knowing your true self.

Jane Martie-Chatlein
Coördinator
SKIN-Rotterdam

*Knowing yourself* is, like the author himself - an honest book! It has a logical build up from a biblical foundation, personal reflections and practical implications. The core message of the book (in my words) is: 'It's there already, God planted it inside you'. It's about being who you are through awareness and choosing to develop yourself by cultivating what is already in you. . If anything, in this time we realise that we cannot design the world as we want it. We can however, in this brokenness come to our potency and 'give space' to who we are deep down, according to Gods purpose with mankind. I recommend this book for anybody who needs reconfirmation about his or her being based on how God meant us to be; balanced in spirit, soul and body. In a unique fashion, this book reflects the author's desire to encourage people to be purpose driven. In the same way he is committed in his role as a board member of SKIN-Rotterdam where he strives to build bridges between churches, government and society, promoting communities to live in unity in diversity of John 17, as well as encouraging international churches to become a powerful voice in society.

Karin de Schipper
Director SKIN-Rotterdam
*Unity, diversity, power*

The desire to make a difference is the highest calling of God. There is a wealth of amazing tools in this book to help you become the instrument of change that you want to be.

The purpose of this book is not to make you a judge of character, but to help facilitate growth in yourself and in others. This understanding may well be the difference between getting to know yourself and becoming better at whatever, you do.

"As for the likeness of their faces, the four had the face of a man, and the face of a Lion, on the right side: and they four had the face of an Ox on the left side; they four also had the face of an eagle" (Ezekiel 1:10).

[7] The first living creature (being) was like a lion, the second living creature like an ox, the third living creature had the face of a man, and the fourth living creature [was] like a flying eagle.

In this scripture, we see mankind in his full glory, colour, and vitality. Man stands in the glory of God in His entire state of power. In this revelation, mankind is expressed as possessing a balance in spirit, soul, and body. He is uncorrupted by the weaknesses of sin and death. He was not contaminated in any way, shape, or form. He is found in the fullness of his original four personalities.

Indeed, in the beginning, man is found reflecting the full power and might of his creator. When we reveal the subject of the personalities of mankind, we are faced with a display of God in love and action. During His creation of mankind, He placed within them the fundamental desire to seek a purpose and the responsibility to carry it out. He pulled out all the stops to adorn mankind with beauty, splendour, and authority. After He had finished, there was nothing else to add; Man was perfect because He had given mankind his best.

## OVERTURE

Someone who knows who they are, is a person who has discovered divine identity, and why they exist. They have as it were, answered the question of the purpose of existence. An answer that undoubtedly resolves the question of purpose, meaning, and happiness. This state will initiate the deep assurance of the persons relevance in society. Most likely, they will be pulled out from that relaxed, and carefree existence, which is often riddled with guess work and the "see-where- the-chips-falls-attitude to life", to a more meaningful, and Impactful living enriching the world around them.

A person who knows who they are, will also understand the world they live in and the world they are meant to live in. This is where their assignment begins. For instance, if you know of a village where there is no electricity, making it hot and unbearable, then your assignment is to make sure there is electricity in that township. Taking this cause qualifies being alive. Jesus put it this way: "For this cause came I to this hour." What is your cause? What is that cause that keeps you awake? Well one way to find that out, comes from the discovery of how personalities work, and function in all kinds of environments.

They say a one-eyed man in the city of the blind automatically becomes its leader. This means that knowing yourself will simply make you a leader wherever you are because you are now able to lead others to also find out who they are.

It is always discouraging, also hurtful to see young men committing various crimes and young women thinking that the only option for success in life, is to offer are their bodies to all sorts of compromising, and questionable lifestyles. These people have grown up believing the wrong information and have stayed too long in a place where the light never comes on.

Someone who knows why they are who they are will be at peace with themselves. There are lots of people living their lives according to what they see in others. There are also people walking around looking for others who they wish to be like. These are copycats, which many become exceptionally good at being!

However, I will suppose that the place, and the power of responsibility means that we take out, valuable time to dig into the crevices of our souls, and to discover the joys of being who we are. It unlocks powerful opportunities that God designed, to empower humans to evolve into something greater than our present reality.

Resolving to becoming a copycat seems to be the most "acceptable" behaviour in current times because most people are tempted at some point in their lives to adapt. There is this strong urge in our society; that says, "we need role models!". It demands response to adaptation in actions and behaviour, by which many have certainly produced desired growth. So, there are times where we must emulate good characteristics such as respect, honour, growth, self-esteem, confidence, or trust. However, we need to develop enough intelligence to know to withdraw from negative propensities such as pride, arrogance, bad habits, disrespect, or confusion.

A person that knows who they are is always conscious and productive with what he or she has. For example, a skilful potter will always acknowledge his gifts and personality in the art of pottery by growing in skill, which will bring him to even higher grounds. Why? This is simply because he is a hundred percent sure he is doing exactly what he was designed to do.

Knowing yourself, your personality, your talents, and your gifts is also one of the important factors of knowing who you are because it inspires what you are willing to develop, both implicitly and explicitly. The drive will become, "how can one manifest potential into realities?" Your personality, when developed, makes you superior. It puts you back in the place of dominion and fulfilment. On the other hand, it can stoke all kinds of inferiority complexes into one's world when ignored. Knowing your personality separates you from the crowd because you now see greatness in you that others are blind to.

Nowadays, it is almost impossible to see successful people who are still in their right minds. Everywhere we turn, we find ourselves wondering how someone could be this rich and famous and still act out of character, yet for some reason command respect. This is simply because true wealth and success begins with knowing who you are and what you have in the inside, and it is quite difficult for most people to understand that money or people cannot tell you who you are.

Finding out who you are is fundamental to living. The moment you do it, you begin to live. It is in this realization that money and the rat race take on a totally different energy. Both become worthless compared to the beauty and value that you have discovered inside.

So now money does not make you rich, you make people rich. Taking a leaf from the experience of Paul the Apostle who wrote most of the new testament of the bible, he puts it this way: "As sorrowful, yet always rejoicing; as poor, yet making many rich; as having nothing, and yet possessing all." So, in no way am I justifying lack as a virtue. On the contrary, I am driving the revelation that there is no one on this planet that possess nothing by which to serve the world. The very fact that one is living connotes that potential is waiting desperately to manifest. Even the "seemingly" weak amongst us, in any community, has the propensity to ignite the creativity of God in all of us.

But Jesus of Nazareth unpacked this concept, while he answered the question concerning a blind boy. He directed the hearts and minds of His disciples, away from the feeling of victimization and toward responsibility. "The boy is not blind because of his or his parent "faults" or sin" says Jesus. Better yet, I want to propose this thought; "why are you concern about problems, when you should be focused on bringing solutions?" Jesus Christ reiterated God's wisdom, stating that sometimes power and strength can be hidden in "seemingly" weak places and the so "called" blindness of the young boy should bring out the best, both in the boy and his instructors.

When a person finds what they have, they cannot help but love themselves and to love especially the God who has intelligently designed them with a purpose, and developing this reality becomes a worthwhile quest. They begin to dream bigger and seek ways of making these dreams a reality.

When personality is discovered and accepted, it reveals paths to advancement, unlike for people who are still focusing on everything they see on the outside or those who still hunger for vain adventures and short expectations.

To acknowledge something means to take notice, to express gratitude, or show appreciation. And is there a better way of expressing love for someone or something than spending time with them? A man who discovers his design can safely turn off the TV, cut off toxic relationships and unreasonable conversations, and spend more time in development. It is like having a relationship that grows intimately the more both parties acknowledge each other.

Personalities are as valuable as gold and as beautiful as diamonds, so the more time and effort you spend polishing them, the more they grow in value and beauty. You can begin to see how valuable and beautiful you are to have such purity and power in you.

## Then Comes Change.

Your gifts and talents now begin to lift you up, changing how you think and feel about yourself, which will determine the kind of company you keep and the places you are willing to go. Your language changes and your value of time and where you spend your energy becomes more selective.

I think it's time we wake up and start seeing ourselves as change instruments and not change seekers. We must be positively changed in order to work out positive changes. We need to take a break and dig deep inside to see what really moves us. If it's money, influence, or fame that moves us, then we're alive but not living because life is priceless. To be able to live, we must discover our priceless personality gifts, talents, and everything that differentiates us from others.

## This Becomes Our Identity.

Identity is important. The question "who are you?" is one of the most difficult and complex questions to answer. Most people who provide an answer misunderstand the context, yet it is an amazingly simple question. Who are you? Is it different from "Where are you from?" or "What do you do?" People tend to give answers like "I am Dutch," or "I am a doctor," or "I am black," which is totally wrong.

You might have been born in Nigeria, which means you also gain the benefit of the land by being identified as a Nigerian, but that doesn't mean you are Nigerian. A doctor is a profession, not an identity. So, saying you are a doctor is like putting yourself in a group of people and saying you all are the same, which is an extremely poor way of thinking. The colour of your skin will only confuse you more, making you to start following, trusting, and honouring the wrong examples in life. It will also separate you from a lot of help from people and positive relationships because of the division of colour you've let into your heart.

## Who Are You?

This question means "What is your name?" because at the end of your life, that is what remains here on Earth, your name. Whether you understand the question or not, if you walked on the Earth, that is who people will remember you as. It also means "What do you stand for?" and "What are you building?" and "What will be your legacy?"

The truth of the matter is that whoever you are is always in the future. It is who you will become. Who you are is strengthened by your cognisance of potential, purpose, and personality. The reason many may struggle with this question is because they wrestle with the present and are blindsided by the miserable inadequacies of the human condition: Therefore, it is sacrifice which forces humans to transcend current limiting conditions to access greater breakthroughs.

## Demand for Sacrifice

A name is not an easy phenomenon to realize, this is simply because of the responsibility and pain the development demands. Today there are names of individuals that have graced this world and they have rightfully left a great and positive impact on our societies indelibly. So, it's appropriate to mention that, the names these individuals answered to, are not merely phonetical arrangement of letters. No! Instead, they trigger in all of us, distinctive feeling of awe, as we remember them. We become reminiscent of their courage, persistence, resilience, and endurance. In their names we remember how these virtues were demonstrated through all kinds of complexities and difficulties. How they responded positively in dire situations because of what they stood for.

## How Joseph made his Name

One case that comes to mind is that of Joseph. In my opinion, Joseph is one character that throughout the period of his life embodied and vividly demonstrated these four-spiritual profiles as discussed in this book.

## The Eagle in Joseph

At a young age he already had clear vision as that of an Eagle. The Eagle personality can see the future clearly from a great distance and on average the Eagle personality is the most meticulous in details and very determined to clarify every step of a project. They are the perfectionist in thinking, can have the aura of superiority based on the strength of the critical nature the Eagle personality exudes, as we shall discuss this further in chapter twenty seven.

So, Joseph knew where he would be, and who he will become in the future. He saw the future from heights that only God can avail to the human soul to foster. He will become a world leader, and very influential. Comparing his influence on that of the sun and the moon, it was so vivid to his spirit, and his mind, and he spoke concerning the future in almost present-day terminology. "someday, my father, my brothers, and the whole world will all come under my care, protection, and preservation, similar to the same power exhibited by the sun and the moon over the earth".

He was one among the twelve sons of Jacob. In the hierarchal structure and dynamics of the family, he was at the bottom of the ladder. You will not be treated lightly with such rhetoric's, especially in a patriarchal hierarchal system, charged with the dominate male behaviours and predispositions for competition and disagreeableness. He would suffer the fate of anyone who challenges the recognised order. As they would be classified, rebels, with a desire to introduce chaos and disruption to the established family structure.

His became statistically the familiar story of rejection, mis-understanding and betrayal by his own brothers. Their hate toward his dreams, led them to conspire against him desiring to kill him by dumping and deserting him in an empty well (Genesis 37:8). In the end, they decided not to commit murder but to sell him off into slavery. Joseph will owe his gratitude to Judah, one of his brothers who thought to intercept this awful murderous plan to the suggestion of selling him off into the slave train of the Ishmaelites. Which is a lesser evil, I suppose. Nonetheless, it is at this stage that Joseph activated the feature of the Man.

## The Man in Joseph

The Man personality is the hyper enthusiastic individual that cannot be easily foiled by the challenges and pessimism of life. He or she thrives in the unknown and will face a variety of challenges life has to throw them. They possess a high sense of flexibility and a keen ability to adapt and adjust, all in a bid not just to survive but to go up triumphing.

Bringing solution to complex problem is second nature for the Man personality, they are recognised for possessing great patience for brainstorming and they function perfect in group dynamics because they see in any situation an opportunity for creativity and solutions.

So, in no time Joseph pivots himself to become relevant to his master by the grace of God that empowers the activation of the strengths in these personalities. As a slave, he landed in the home of Potiphar, an officer to Pharaoh, and the captain of the guard. Joseph's enthusiasm, adaptability, and ability to generate relevant solutions for his master plus certainly the spiritual edge of Gods favour, propelled Joseph to the top of the rank and he became the head of Potiphar's home and businesses in the end.

He grew to be the best in the household of his master, by this time the scriptures revealed how he prospered. This always gets me thinking; "how can a slave prosper so much, that it becames headlines? (Genesis 39:2),". One cannot over emphasis the power of knowing yourself. Even as a slave he was loved by his master (Genesis 39:4), which again is a quality of the Man personality. The Man personality are lovable people, harmless and are relentlessly supportive.

In principle this admirable quality can be misrepresented by others. They can be misconstrued in their intentions to be self-seeking at many levels and may attract unwelcomed attention from that may not be convenient to the Man personality.

In the case of Joseph being that absolute mature specimen of personality, he evolved to using the dominate Lion personality to his advantage at this point.

## The lion in Joseph

The point where Potiphar's wife misread all the signs of Joseph's servitude to be compliance to whatever comes, was an error. She wanted more from Joseph than his daily chores and responsibilities. She wanted to have an intimate relationship with Joseph, which is simply a bad idea, judging from what will happen to him for touching his master's wife. Higher from this objection in his mind was the plan of God and Gods higher purpose for his life, which nothing would stop him from achieving.

This is the language of the Lion personality showing up at the right time in Joseph's walk of adversity. It is the language of persistence, resilience, relentlessness, and fearlessness. Which never gives up the focus on the goal. Joseph had received a vision and goal and the Lion personality would switch on to empower his toe-to-toe fight with any force intending to redirect the manifestation of his potential and purpose. This Lion personality enforced his courage to say no to Potiphar's wife despite the consequence that would follow. Wrongly accused of tampering with the lady, he was thrown into prison for a period.

It will be great to interject here, and to specify that during his prison sentence we see the personality of Man again in play here, because not for long he was spotted by the guards for being the most cheerful, harmless, and enthusiastic fellow that he was. So much so that the keys to the prison was handed over to him and the charge of the other prisoners were placed in Joseph's care (Genesis 39:22) he may do as he wishes. Is not this admirable? The fact that the gloom and doom of the prison environment could not dampen Joseph, who resolved to remain enthused with his God given vision.

This Lion personality will manifest later again in his story. This is referring to when he was released from prison after being summoned to Pharaoh's palace. He was confronted with the dreams of Pharaoh. The Lion's boldness to stand before

Pharaoh with the nerve to master the already tensed atmosphere of aggression and intimidation coming from Pharaoh's magicians and enchanters, who had claimed they could also interpret dreams but at this point had failed at all attempts. Joseph was not intimidated by their presence, but with confidence and courage interpreted all of Pharaoh's dreams.

The following personality was the strength that powered Joseph's next level of success, catapulting him to the top in the realms of the Egyptian empire. Joseph's courage positioned the world in a way where it could survive the impending worldwide draught by the maximization of the next Personality which is revealed in the Ox.

## The Ox in Joseph

The Ox is so special a personality. This was Joseph's premium personality that worked all along to stabilize him through all his adversity. So that if the Lion was instrumental in securing Joseph a place as God helped Egypt, then it is the Ox that will sustain his reign.

The ox is that secure, stable, satisfied, and that angelic like personality. They possess a grateful, and a kind disposition, but one incredibly special attribute about the ox is they are extremely resourceful. Joseph, functioning in an Ox personality is given the audacious task to lead this never-seen-before-project that would become the hallmark in agriculture until today. It will go down in history as the movement that secure the future of an empire and the world at large.

This can only take the patience and the productivity of the Ox. The work ethics of the ox and the stable character cannot be compared with the rest of the four personalities. Because part of the feature in the dream of pharaoh was to secure a seven-year of abundance and then make sure that the abundance of crop is sustained and preserved to provide food and trade for the entire empire, for the next seven years of austerity. So, systems of irrigation farming had to be introduced to the world to increase crop productivity, and silos were invented to preserve crop from the elements, and they had to be built all in record time. One of the main qualities of the Ox is, it's ability to work. And work did Joseph, until all Egypt celebrated the gift of God in their midst.

Many will prefer not to take such responsibility and suffer under the continuous strain of mistaken identity and confusion. It takes a thorough understanding of the context of sacrifice to have access to this answer. Sacrifice helps the process. You can answer this question by asking certain questions about sacrifice.

Sacrifice is all about improving the future. You always need to give up something to receive another. Life is designed that way. Many suffer from rejection, but the upside is that life would not work without rejection. So, at nine months, the womb rejects the baby because it is time. It might be a painful process, but the revelation is that without sacrifice, both the baby and the mother would be in danger.

Who do I see in the future and what am
I willing to give up to get it?
What is my attitude toward self-discovery?
What is the personality type I need to embrace?
What behavioural adjustment do I need?

You must understand that all the personalities God created are designed to improve the future. They are fundamental for advancing humanity to ultimately improve existence. They are fundamental to human fulfilment and universal good.

The questions above are unending but the answer to each is determined by your courage to sacrifice all temporal pleasure to improve the future. So, how willing are you to give up, to reach a greater awareness of your God-created personality?

The concept of sacrifice allows you to understand the divine reasons for manifesting potential for a better future. Sacrifices are like self-imposed prison sentences to incarcerate those unruly, appetite-seeking indulgence in reckless and retrogressive behaviours. One makes sacrifices to wilfully enslave that tempter of human weakness and reasons not to take responsibility for time, potential, and opportunities for personal discipline. It enslaves it, as it were, and puts it behind the bars of intentionality and plain hard work.

Again, Paul, The Apostle, introduces these charges to us as he stamps his foot and draws a line in the sand, showing us how he took full responsibility for the advancement of excellence in his life and ministry. "No, I discipline my body and make it my slave, so that after I have preached to others, I myself will not be disqualified" (1 Corinthians 9:27).

Most people are still not stepping up to answer the question of identity and have yet to respond to the call from inside regarding these four personalities. It may be because of the families they come from, issues of low self-esteem, ignorance, or because they have lost hope in the journey of becoming all they want to be.

The strength of the beauty that comes from inside is that you know how good and precious you are and what you have from God, and that he has made these identities clear to you. Nobody can mislead you anymore because they can see the difference in you.

I sincerely hope that you actualize all you set your heart to do in the strength and design of your creator. By going through this book, you have earned your self-success and become a change instrument.

Pastor Alexander Emoghene
Lead Pastor Claypot church international

# PART 1

# Something Went Wrong

*The effects of Sin*

The imperfection that entered humanity through the first family engineered the loss of our complete self-cognizance. This imperfection is called sin (Genesis 2:17).

Another phrase that helps to fully understand the word "sin" is "missing the mark." All humanity was stored as potential winners in the seed of Adam. Humanity is destined to emerge as perfect beings in full demonstration of the power and glory, as revealed in the four personalities.

But when sin entered through the decision of the first couple, it led humanity to miss the mark of this high calling and tumble down the path of self-ignorance and God-ignorance.

Firstly, the implication of their decision was that they were cut off from their life source, making it impossible to function in the fullness of these grand personalities. Secondly, this choice evolved into all the abnormalities, brokenness, and loneliness we experience in our world today. Thirdly, it created a void and the exhaustive search for where we belong.

Therefore, we must struggle through the uncertainties, doubts, fears, indecision, and faults of life to reach a satisfactory place. Many have ascended to great heights through training and the empowerment of mind and have created vast wealth and resources. Yet, they still feel deprived of the knowledge of who they are in God.

Recently, we have heard of very wealthy people who tragically ended it all by taking their lives. These are individuals who believe in the alluring message of having, growing the joys and pleasures of what we all consider successful.

Humanity lost the ability to function with all four personalities at the same time. Thus, we began to operate far lower than our design, causing an average human to work with only two of these personalities—a primary and a secondary.

The good news is that redemption gives us access to divine empowerment, weaponizing our souls with the revelation of these four personalities to uncover the power locked within us. Hence the recovery and restoration of our divine image can become a reality.

You can develop a complete use of the four personalities in time to help you, whenever and wherever you may need them. You may not become perfect and robust in the function that the four personalities possess. However, you have the amazing opportunity to release the full potential of your primary personalities and grow to utilize your desired persona.

# CHAPTER 2

# In the Process

*The Concept of Brokenness*

I am sure you have heard the phrase "brokenness before the Lord," or maybe found yourself using it. The first cause of this brokenness is the separation from God. The second cause is the pressure of life's rat race—the struggle to achieve.

I am sometimes curious by the word translators use for "broken" (such as "shabar" in Hebrew), which was captured in Psalms 51:17: "The sacrifices of God are a broken spirit: a broken and a contrite heart, O God, thou wilt not despise."

So, the word "broken" in this text illustrates a heart which is torn apart or shattered. It speaks of one who is heartbroken because of one reason or another. It could be through disappointments, a bitter divorce, the loss of a loved one, bankruptcy, self-inflicted pain, and the list goes on...

Well, the scripture invites such persons to God for an encounter with His healing. The worshipper is reassured that no matter what, God will not despise them.

I like how the Cambridge dictionary defined the word "despise" as *"to feel a strong dislike for someone or something because you think that the person or thing is bad or has no value."*

This sums up the first concept of brokenness regarding knowing your personality traits from the divine perspective. God comes to the place of brokenness to render help in times of need.

There is something in humanity that likes to present our best face. We love to put on that poker face of strength, courage, and persistence. These attitudes can get you a long way, but you will still eventually get to the place where you will need God for healing and deliverance. Maybe you are there now?

In times of true brokenness, He wants to be near us, if only we could take off our masks before him. God is not really looking for a perfect man; He is a perfect God with the remedy for a broken humanity.

The second concept of brokenness is found within the complexity of defining the word "brokenness." In this definition, the study of divine personality truly comes alive.

It refers to the occasion of breaking forth—meaning the good things trapped inside you will burst into existence, giving birth to something new.

This brings out something that was not there beforehand so a person may come into alignment and find their purpose. After all the obstacles of life, this person has been trained by these same circumstances and come out better off and victorious. This is brokenness; it refers to someone who is trained for success and not necessarily getting tired or feeling like a victim but went intentionally to become a leader in any industry.

This definition is derived from the art of breaking a horse to be made future-fit and battle-ready. This was in the olden days, of course. Nowadays, the military fires guided missiles from the comfort of home. In the early times, horses and chariots were the weapons of war.

However, the techniques for breaking a horse have not evolved much, other than becoming more refined due to better animal rights laws which prevent animal abuse. So, this flashback is purely for emphasis.

In times past, it is said that horses, especially horses ridden into battle by kings, would have been put through rigorous drills such as riding slowly through rapid rivers or standing over fire. Through all this, the horse is resilient and courageous in the face of fear and pain. Any horse that pulls through these tests will be called a broken horse.

Brokenness is the stage where individuals align themselves to explore the glory, power, and majesty of the service of God.

This horse could be called upon in battle to serve its master. It is willing to confidently break out onto a new horizon, and as it strives to get better, it is driven by humility and obedience.

So, knowing that your divine personality is like giving birth to the real you that flows with God's divine purpose, outperforming and out classing your own efforts, you must become a broken person before God. This is the point at which you are introduced to yourself. You then enter the fullness of all God has equipped you to accomplish. So, in this concept, brokenness is a total surrender at the discovery of what God created.

In other words, just as the horse serves its rider, you become more aware of yourself, the way you have been designed by God, the purpose He has given you, and the path toward that purpose. You become your best form in the spirit, and you are called a broken believer before God.

# This Is For All

*Major Characteristics of the Four Personalities*

For I am not ashamed of the gospel, because it is the
power of God that brings salvation to everyone who
believes: first to the Jew, then to the Gentile.
—Romans 1:16

Typically, people promptly ask, "Do I have just one of these personalities, or do I possess more? Can a single individual possess all four personalities?"

As we alluded, the scripture reveals that man was made in the likeness of God (Genesis 1:26).

It is from this blueprint that we get the reference for the four faces of man. Let us take a closer look at the mystery in the creation of man.

"…also, out of the midst thereof came the likeness of four living creatures. And this was their appearance; they had the likeness of a man" (Ezekiel 1:5).

There are four types of personalities that explain the inherent qualities that the God of creation lavished on every individual, so each can excel wherever they find themselves in life (Genesis 1:26).

This intricate design confirms the unique difference attributed to the human family in contrast to the rest of creation. These personality types reveal the uniqueness of creativity, innovation, inventions, initiatives, development, and diversity of growth found exclusively in the human family.

This privilege is given to all individuals to accept the grand plan of God. The secular establishments have created many seminars, training programs, and conferences about personality profiling to create positions and harmony in the workplace. They have made many believe that through simple pie charts, they can prove whether they are in their place of power or not. But by God's design and standards, we prove that these personalities are buried in all for the benefit of all. So, it depends on your ability to believe the truth.

Some of us will have to deliberately break boxes to fully enter our place of power. You will need to make radical changes to accept the new you. And it will all be worth it. There's more to you than meets the eye. The question is, are you ready to do more?

Purposeful change is often very taxing because everything will become new. Many want to become new, and we pray to become new, but subconsciously set ourselves up to continue manifesting the past.

I mean, our environment mostly reminds us to lean into the past; past friends, past celebrations, past pictures on our mobile devices, past images on our walls in our homes. We call these memories or "walking down memory lane." We recount past failures, past regrets, or even past successes.

Remember how powerful your mind is. Memories are seeds. The purpose of a seed is to sprout, and it wants to manifest. I like to make this power statement: "You cannot find an old seed which has lost the will to sprout." As soon as it finds the right environment, it will sprout. Old seeds need the compost of the past, while new seeds need the compost of future thinking.

You need your mind to believe that your future is better than what you see now. So, what are you loaded with? This is a game of influence; the loudest voice in you will influence your decisions and, eventually, your results. Therefore, it will take a conscious and concerted mind shift to believe something new and better about you.

Let's go deeper in the next chapter to uncover the nature of this upstream battle. I used the word "upstream" because all the changes you require in your life naturally feel like swimming upstream. They will take strategic thinking and courage to stay in the flow until you win.

⚘



# CHAPTER 4

# "...Then We Can Soar!"

*Environmental Conditions*

There is a story that's popular with motivational speakers—you may have heard it before. It is the story of an eagle that was raised by a flock of ducks. Throughout his young life, he believed he was a duck. One day, at the pond where the flock often quenched their thirst, there came an eagle who landed for a brief drink. This young eagle had never seen a sight like this, and he was struck with curiosity.

*I look just like this guy!* he thought.

Before he could gather himself, he saw—as in a dream—how this eagle lifted effortlessly into the air. He was not flapping franticly and awkwardly like the ducks. He was stronger and smoother, and with just a few flaps, he mounted great heights.

With a majestic wing, off he soared into the open skies. Needless to say, the young eagle's life was transformed that day. He was raised by the wrong parents, and now he had encountered his real nature.

It would be a very ungrateful thing to dismiss the struggle that our parents went through to bring us up. To some fortunate ones, their parents are superheroes. Others may not feel as blessed because they were neglected or raised by Uncle PlayStation and Aunt Social Media.

Nonetheless, most of the time, we still find ourselves inadequately prepared for our assignments; hence, the preaching of the Gospel's good news. The Gospel brings the believer into a place of total restoration, where the mind of God is revealed. With this awareness, we can all find our true design and identity. Then we can soar!

Our upbringings are often the first port of hindrance to our discovery. Imagine an eagle being raised by, let's say, a broken eagle.

A broken eagle may be equivalent to an underachieving parent; a bird who could not develop themselves properly enough to fly at great heights. In the long run, he will pass this inability down to his offspring.

Though eagles possess the potential to fly high, this young eagle will be exposed to a life of mediocrity, devoid of excellence. It's likely that his parents will only lead him to become critical against flying, to make excuses about why they should maintain low altitudes, or to declare how they are simply not like other eagles ("We are incredibly careful because of the up and down drafts").

You can relate this to all the other personality profiles and how the next generations are prepared to face the challenges before them.

$$\infty$$

CHAPTER 5

# "...Untamed...

*Parental Gift Disposition and Upbringing*

The word "environmental" is a compound word because it contains two words. "Environ," which relates to what's around you, joins with "mental," which relates to the mind. Simply put, the culture we create reflects what surrounds us. Lions in the wild have a different attitude compared to lions in cages at zoos. Have you found the environment for your personality? Do you need to be released into the "wild" where your personality can thrive?

An environment truly determines how gifts are nurtured and deployed. On an early date with my wife, I showed her a picture of my mother.

"You look like your mum!" she exclaimed.

*If you only had a clue,* I thought.

Our family is large and mostly made up of boys, so we took turns playing, fighting, and sporting—particularly indoor football. We drove mum mad. Years later, as I count down my nine siblings from one mum, I can truly testify to how different in disposition we all are. Our upbringing was one of poverty, lack, and deprivation.

Being brought up in such conditions made it necessary to develop an unhealthy survival spirit, which manifested in greed and stinginess. This disposition was counter intuitive to my primary personality, which was to be generous and giving. This study is helping me grow out of the limitations my upbringing instilled in me.

> *"...become broken enough to follow your dreams..."*

So, in my formative environment, due to the suppressive surroundings, the situation tamed my instincts as it were, that came with my primary personality which is, to share and care for others.

Being tamed simply means to control something dangerous or powerful. Life can take a malevolent turn due to one's upbringing which tames your primary personality from reaching its full potential. Your personality contains all you need to combat and compete in this life as observed in this study, I am referring to the Godly agency in your personality for becoming a success.

It took a long time for me to figure out my personality traits. I was jammed by many other influences and ended up neglecting who I really was. Because I was discouraged from discovering the blessings and strength buried in my personality type, I could not become broken enough to follow my dreams, until the Lord commenced the restoration process in my heart to commensurate to the destiny I hold.

# CHAPTER 6

# "…The Blessing of Poverty"

*Social Conditions*

Research shows that children raised in poverty are more driven to bring about positive change in the world than their rich counterparts would be. This is what I call the blessing of poverty. Yes, it is ironic, I know. You're probably asking how poverty can bring blessings.

Look around you. Statistics show that there are more self-made individuals than individuals who inherited their wealth. The stories of these self-made individuals often tell of the struggles of life and how they had to build everything from the bottom up.

Social class causes a lot of derailment of purpose and loss of precious lives full of talent. Many will function totally different if they could only be found in different social conditions. Yet, it is in these dire conditions in the human experience that you find great turn around stories of rags to riches played out in the most amazing fashion.

Spiritual sin separated humanity from our original social environment, which is fellowship with divinity. In this social connection, God's chosen words were used to build the human spirit. Words such as blessings, replenish, multiple, increase, and greatness. God said, "Let us make man in our image and likeness." The word of God, formed the fundamental structure by which human beings, find their natural resilience to fights against contrary conditions.

This is our original social condition, connection, and network in God. And so, redemption brings this switch and takes humanity into its original social construct. It empowers the believer to change spiritual, emotional, and social platforms. To break whatever prevents these divine personalities from manifesting. As we realize the power of that potential, they will break the lies of social class and transcend all barriers for a better life in God.

✌



# CHAPTER 7

# "...I Do Not Want It!"

*Generational Curse*

When I was young, there was a mentally challenged man who spent every evening loitering up and down the marketplace, being chased by one retailer or the other. He would usually beg for food or money, and I remember how we would run behind him and tease him, which would make him frantic after a while. I am not proud about that behaviour, even as a kid.

Why tell this story? I learnt very quickly that whatever was on this man, I did not want it. I often wonder what had happened to him in his early days. Even as a child, I began to feel we needed to stop teasing him, otherwise what was on him would pass to us. Frightening, I know!

This is what the curse or the blessing really is, in practical terms. The blessing is better defined as being empowered to prosper with God. In my story, I felt if what was on the mentally challenged man was passed on to us, we would be caused or empowered to fail. That is how the curse operates; it empowers individual to fail or fall out of God.

Sin brought a curse to the human system. After Adam and Eve went astray, the door of their disobedience opened and allowed all that came over the human family.

These curses ruled over humanity, making sure that we could not function in the fullness of the glory of God. The scripture talks about how man has sinned and fallen short of God's glory. In another place, the scripture calls mankind the glory of God. It further implies that mankind, having been made in the image of God, fell off that standard, and now without God's image in man, we could only function lower than God's design.

The discovery of your personality type is a deterrent against the curse. When you discover your personality gift, you will break existing curses and new curses will not be able to find a landing spot in your life.

CHAPTER 8

# Scaling of Possibilities

*Your Dreams are Calling for Manifestation*

Possibilities makes life beautiful. Humanity can freely operate in all these glorious divine personalities and gifting. Through deliberate efforts to nurture, and to develop these personalities, we to capture the beauty of each personality is released.

For example, your primary personality might be the Ox. You may feel that you are a gentle soul and very satisfied in your present environment. Yet, for some reason, you feel there is more to your life, and you really do not have the agency to push the boundaries. The dream in you is calling for manifestation, and you must realize that by pushing the boundaries, your level of excellence and achievement will change.

In this quagmire, you need the Lion personality. The Lion personality is a goal-oriented and persistent personality that pushes past obstacles to get the job done.

But for a gentle, stable, and loving soul, this may come off as uncouth and unnecessary behaviour that an Ox personality would never adopt.

Understand, however, that what the Lion personality provides is not bossing people around or having your way. Later in the book, we shall deal with the weakest of all the personalities, where being bossy and uncouth happens to be one of the weaknesses of a broken Lion personality.

For now, we are talking about a healthy desire for growth and how to set realistic goals and executing them. A primary Ox personality will resist aggressive change, believing that advancement ought to be a natural way of life. Meanwhile, the Lion in you will keep you moving forward until the job gets done. So, you can realize the amazing opportunities the Lion personality could create for you as you engage in your life-improvement goals.

# CHAPTER 9

# The Vision Question

*Living by Design*

Though it is not the purpose of this book, you cannot consider this topic without treading on the heart of vision.

As you have noticed, the four personalities possess one thing in common, which is the eye. All four personalities are driven by vision. They may vary in power, but they all hold unique vantage points. The personality is a drive to fulfill an assignment of our various lives. Without the discovery of these gifts, many visions will be frustratingly unrealized.

Vision needs the fuel called motivation, and finding the right motivation is crucial. It takes a clear knowledge of your personality. Think of it like eating the proper meals to keep you healthy and energized; An ox is herbivorous, a lion is carnivorous, and man is omnivorous.

The question is, which of these creatures are you? And what are you feeding on? And does it have the right nutrient to power up the dream machine in you?

Vision is having a picture of your preferred future, but it takes the right motivation, character, and brokenness to see any vision advance from dreams to reality. It is one thing to see where you need to be, but another thing to have the tenacity, courage, values, and the strength of character needed to get there. And once you are, it takes different sets of skill to stay there.

The awareness of our divine design helps to light the way, like a beacon of hope, to lead all our inner dreams and assignments to manifest as individuals or teams.

Some people may be good at seeing the future, but for one reason or another, they fail to manifest their vision. Others may just need that extra helping hand to navigate their way to success. Whichever you may be, your divine design will play a pivotal role.

# PART 2

# CHAPTER 10

# Finding the Right Life Partner

Finding the right partner has always been the challenge for single people. "How do I know he is the right one? Is this God's will for me? Am I ready to commit? Why do I feel afraid each time I am approached? I want to do this once and for all! I do not want to be disappointed. I was hurt in my previous relationship and now, so I am so careful. I do not think anyone will ever love me. I am not attractive enough. I feel ready, but no one is here for me. Where is the right person?"

We can go on and on with these beautiful moments of frustrating anticipation. Many ask these questions in monologue, but they should instead engage in a dialogue with the God in us.

What you should actually be asking yourself are the "blessings questions." If you cannot bless the one you are with, you may not find fulfillment in that relationship. Otherwise, you may deceive yourself into finding someone to meet only your needs, leaving the other person empty after they have poured out all they have into you.

So, these are some "blessings questions" to consider: How can I be a blessing to the one that will come into my life?

How best can I ensure they come alive when they find me?

How can I become the best to help them fulfill their purpose?

What personality best serves us as we head toward our glorious future?

Discovering your divine personality types helps one to answer these life-changing questions. It is human nature to be self-serving until they find a cause for which they can really make a difference. The Man personality, for example, is wired to motivate, inspire, and innovate. They just need to find a partner with a clear vision for their future, like an entrepreneur. Someone with a dream and the Man personality will be in marriage heaven. If you have an unclear picture of your primary personality, you might make a choice that disrupts who you really are.

# CHAPTER 11

# Finding the Right Carrier

We derive the word "career" from the intent of carrying something valuable that serves the need of others. What you carry in your personality type is a powerful gift given by God to meet certain needs of humanity. We can judge this by the fact your dream is not often self-serving because when dreams are fulfilled, there are always beneficiaries that will enjoy the fruits of your labour.

What is the right career for you? In other words, what are you born to carry? What can you accomplish in life? What will you find more joyful doing? So often, many try living a life of finding and studying for a career. Not to discourage pursuing self-development, but our education system should become more strategic to adjust its goal to feeding either the Ox, Lion, Eagle, or Man personality types in students. We should inspect our primary personality gifts for clues and confidence.

In India, I gathered from several *TED Talks* presenters that many questions have been raised about their education system—a dated framework of their British colonial past. The narrative is that the system was built simply to educate individuals to serve the growing industrial revolution in the west. They were not allowed to explore personal talents, nor were they encouraged to apply others forms of creativity, except for within the frame of working in a factory or carrying out secretarial jobs.

An Ox, for example, would have found peace if they had been educated early in life about what would be the right career for them. So, they should have been allowed to realize that they'd do best in a peaceful working environment—one which is less competitive and more hospitable and caring.

If only they had been instructed this way earlier, they would have flourished in a stable, predictable environment instead of joining the rat race of the Lion or Man's personality and trying to be forceful and competitive.

If the Ox personality is not sent in the right direction, they end up shattering from within and needing restoration. In the *TED Talks*, it is concluded that the pressure to compete in this narrow path has led to alarming suicide rates among young students.

So, what are you carrying? Once you can identify what you carry, you have an indication of what your potential career will be. This will be your motivation to live from the inside out.

I call this living with the hindsight in mind. In other words, we should see your income in life, whether it be financial or social, as a picture of how much you discover and maximize your outcomes.

Ultimately, we are rewarded in life because of the value we bring to the table. By learning to become authentic, we become more valuable to society and the world around us. We will not be destroyed by what we carry; rather, what we carry will be a channel for blessing. The greatest teacher that ever lived on the Earth, Jesus Christ, put it this way: "Out of your belly shall flow rivers of living water." The question is, have you recovered your river yet?

# CHAPTER 12

# Choosing the Right Business

This can be like finding the right career, but this is a question of entrepreneurship. There is this understanding that some are more gifted than others. While there is truth to this statement, the scripture reveals that all the personalities possess power of vision.

Vision, in many respects, will create enterprise, and when enterprise is put to the test, it grows into the opportunity for entrepreneurship. So, we can take a housewife, for example, with the skill set of baking cupcakes. She only needs to become more and more enterprising by selling a little here and there starting from her relatives and friends. Before you know it, word gets around, and she can develop a cupcake business.

The presupposition that a well-developed divine personality type does not have the potential to become a global leader in their sphere of influence can be misleading. Leadership is inspired and resourced at the point where purpose is discovered. The backdrop to this misleading premise may be due to that fact that the personalities are featured in a clear dichotomy to each other. Meaning two are listed as followers in disposition and the other two are listed as leaders in disposition, thereby instigating and leading some individuals to conclude that they are not leaders and that some are designed for leadership.

The idea is not in no way, shape, or form to portray one of these personalities to be subservient to the another. Much to their uniqueness, it is to show how all personalities have been positioned to fit their various assignments, and how they all can work in perfect union which each other in mankind. So, it depends which vantage point the individual is being approached by challenges or the unknown, will determine which personality get activated. In which case, enough resource or defences will be generated for the individual, with the necessary wisdom and solutions that marches up to their challenges.

Let us take the Eagle personality. In our quadrant, we see the Eagle depicted as featured as the Follower's personality type. But let us look at a bald eagle in nature, which is built to soar majestically up to heights of 10,000–15,000 feet. It can reach 60–80 miles per hour while diving to snatch its prey. A standard human's sight is 20/20, but an eagle's is 20/4, which means it can see up to five times further than any human.

(www.improveeyesighthq.com/eagle-eyesight.html)(www.reference.com/pets-animals/high-can-eagle-fly)

Can you imagine an individual with a primary inclination as an Eagle? As an Eagle personality just starting out in his or her carrier path, enthused with lots of hope and aspiration for success. I suspect this dream has the potential to becoming a reality. judging from the abilities possessed by the Eagle's personality, as we shall understand in later chapters. Eagle personalities has the potential to reach great heights in whatever field they find themselves in. People with the primary gift of the Eagle have a heightened sense of precision, and excellence. Profession where Eagles have the propensity to find the right environment can include architecture, aviation, Information and technology, and engineering. They often are high achievers with zero tolerance for errors, and shoddy work.

So, any enterprise in which the Eagle engages must stimulate and inspire these natural inclinations, or else they may become a flightless, critical, and grumpy old Eagle.

If you need to set out as an entrepreneur, ask questions about the nature of your desired field. Ask what type of people that field attracts and see if you could find your flow among them. If you still wish to enter this field, you have at least done your due diligence and are more aware of what partner you will need. This individual will have either a primary type or a secondary type that will rightly balance out your deficiencies.

CHAPTER 13

# Developing Entrepreneurial Skill

I believe that anybody can be trained to manifest their dreams. The keyword is "train." As mentioned in chapter four, where I alluded to the premise that getting to "soar" in life as it were, come by answering the environmental question rather than biological. It therefore reinforces the importance of responding to the challenge of skill development. And how powerful would it be, when a person decides to take on the challenge of strategic training? "Just as you are doing right now reading this book." Each personality created by God is designed to arrive at a place of fulfillment and success. I use the word success, from a deeper, and introspective standpoint. I am not just referring and clamouring for the attainment of the material aspect of life, which of course brings along its temporal incentive to happiness. Rather, it is much more the durable and longer lasting virtues that humanity thrives on, that which when released affects, molds and, shapes the lives of future generations.

If it is not your destiny, then it will not be buried deep in you and you will not have the urge to become an instrument of change. The problem in many cases is the unwillingness to face how we are designed on the inside and a failure to accept the right nurture needed to develop those specific personality traits. When you can confront and answer these two fundamental concepts, you will find that consuming the information needed to excel will become more palatable.

Unfortunately, we often look over our neighbours' fence to enjoy a panoramic view of how developed they are in persons, process, and power. We romance the idea of "if I could only develop myself like that..." It is wise to consider that those neighbours may be enjoying the benefits of discovering their primary personality.

For example, as a Lion, they can now feed and empower themselves the Lion way. They understand the purpose of success from the Lion's perspective and are willing to be trained as a Lion, a very hands-on approach that can be heavy and rough, yet with lots of love. An Ox that gets inspired by the development process of a Lion may not want to study the benefit of growth from the Lion but needs to find the Ox way of development instead.

Subsequently, developing skill is all about weaponizing individual purposes for superior performance. The upskill concept is the driving force for sustainable growth and the courage to engage in any enterprise. Upskill can be costly and may require accepting a shift into new paradigms. When we operate in our primary personality type, the process is sustainable until results begin to show. When you are clear about your personality gifts and what staple food and tools are needed for sustainable growth, any of these personalities could rise to become a force of high-impact leadership.

# CHAPTER 14

# Raising Children

There is a common saying: "Parenting does not come with a manual." Parenting, like many other processes, has continuously evolved through the ages. From the more traditional family units of father, mother, and children, we have experienced progressively more colourful constructs to the family unit.

The focus here is not so much about the family unit (of which I am a traditionalist when it comes to the family establishments), but more about what efforts the society is ready to render unto the next generation and how this generation will be encouraged to perpetuate and build healthy families. This is the crux of the matter.

Research shows the impact family can have on the upbringing of an individual. Leaving a generation that is highly developed behind to lead to future change and add value to life should be any community's drive.

I sometimes imagine an education system that is tailor-made to address the issue of precision education and to teach the basis of primary personalities, as opposed to the one-size-fits-all system in many schools around the world. Although a challenge like this can require major costs to run, such as a big financial stress, structure of new facilities, and teachers, an experiment of this nature can make all the difference in the lives of the next generation.

Take bald eagles for example, which stay in the nest for around eight to twelve weeks before they are ready to fledge. Their upbringing is far different than the lion. Eagles are just as ferocious of hunters as Lions, yet the growth process of the lion is much slower. After six weeks, the mother lion brings her cub out of the den, where it had been totally reliant on the mother's rich milk for its nourishment. In addition, the cub remains under the mother's protection for one year before venturing out on their own as adults. So, you can agree that as strong as the personality of the lion, their growth to adulthood is so different than the eagle.

Meanwhile, through an in-depth look at the calf, we discover she is weaned in just six to eight weeks. What's impressive is that they begin to eat grass within the first week. This is startling, because in most descriptions of the Ox personality, they are not shown in this light. Often, we are unaware of how quickly the development in a young individual with an Ox personality can be. They can advance in attitude and character far quicker than the other personality types. One reason is that the Ox personality thrives in order and structure; they are eager to follow instructions and accomplish tasks. Most young Ox personalities become self-sufficient before any of the other personalities.

Therefore, the Ox personality is often taken for granted as being the satisfied, stable, and gentle. Their parents may say, "I just do not see a drive in my child."

However, the parent with a robust understanding of their personality will be thrilled to have a child that is fast to wean and willing to take instructions and will grow in strength. The Ox is their best child, a gem, and very admirable because they are kind and obedient, though may look little timid and unassuming at first. They are always saying yes, love taking instruction, and are not confrontational. But a child like this can be passed off as unexciting, slow, and a push-over.

Under the right parental guidance, however, the Ox personality is mostly early bloomers. They build fast muscles for life and very resilient to change. They flourish in the routine and daily structure of living. They may not be boisterous, outgoing, or the life of the party, like the Lion or the Man personalities, but in the right environment, the Ox personality will surely stand out in the crowd.

Therefore, understanding the personality types, we will appreciate each child and render our proper focus on better upbringing methods and education styles.

## DEAL LEARNING ENVIRONMENT

| Left | Right |
|---|---|
| Face of Man (The Leader) | Face of Ox (The Follower) |
| Functional | Instructional |
| Fast Changes | Inspirational |
| Formative | Intimate |
| Futuristic | Imitative |
| Face Lion (The Leader) | Face of Eagle (The Follower) |
| Challenging | Attentive |
| Corrective | Adaptive |
| Confrontational | Attractive |

# CHAPTER 15

# Working Under Stressful Conditions

Research shows that stress is the number one cause of several illnesses and is even deadly at times. Many have attributed the source of stress to the workplace. Many Gallup polls show how companies carry out regular updates on their respective EAPs (Employee Assistance Program) to try and protect their worker's mental health and prevent other stress-related challenges.

Gallup polls points to a unique challenge following the rise of working remotely. Data shows that there are several advantages to this new arrangement, such as commute time being drastically reduced, more customizable work environments, and of course parents being able to spend more time with their families. However, more people are getting disconnected from the culture of their workplace. They feel unappreciated and undervalued because the effort they put into their work goes unnoticed. This is introducing the workplace to new kinds of stress.

This is a perfect time to begin to know yourself and ask the right question and align your vision concerning your assignment on life. Stress is a perfect indication of positioning. It is like a lion in the zoo versus a lion in the wilds. They are the same in disposition, but one is positioned in the right environment, where its potential has room to fully develop.

Can you imagine what would happen to you if you find and work from your natural professional habitat? Where the stress of everyday life does not sway you from living with purpose? Living and working in your right habitat will turn your mundane activities into the most adventurous projects ever. Since the workplace is where you spend the best part of your life, wouldn't you rather do so through your divine personality instead of bending to fit another set of cultures?

| LEFT | RIGHT |
| --- | --- |
| <u>Face of Man (The Leader)</u><br><br>MAN<br><br>Lots of Room for flexibility, and creativity, Innovation, and disruption environment | <u>Face of Ox (The Follower)</u><br><br>High Productive environment with scheduling.<br><br>Long term and achievable goals<br><br>Labour-intensive environment |
| <u>Face Lion (The Leader)</u><br><br>Planned and achievable goal-oriented environment.<br><br>Short term and low labour-intensive environment | <u>Face of Eagle (The Follower)</u><br><br>Managerial and focus driving projects.<br><br>High stress levels with define goals-oriented environment. |

# CHAPTER 16

# Finding Where to Live

I lived in London for the best part of my teenage years and my twenties. I flourished in the UK. I like the hustle and bustle; the people from different backgrounds all converge in this melting pot of a city. I really like the innovations and creativity that city life forces out of people. Of course, it is not all glitz and glamour, but cities have a way of creating commerce and enterprise that blesses the community around it.

Directed to start a church in Rotterdam in early 2000, my wife and I were to live in the Netherlands for the missions. This was a real challenge when we arrived, as it was a smaller city than London. It was uninspiring, thus no help making sense of our call to ministry, and it was all mundane. We felt so detached, but faith in God and an understanding of our divine personality played a strong role in our resilience, and we now feel more established both as a family and ministry.

The role your divine personality plays in your work should not be underestimated. It will determine if you make it out there or not. Working really means growth. So, the question is if you are growing at your location or place of your work.

Many prefer to silence the inner voice of destiny because of the threatening screech from the security of a region rather than asking the question of location.

There is a place for you, and one of the best ways to determine it is through your personality gifting. Eagles are designed for high altitude; that is where they come alive. It needs the updraft and the downdraft to thoroughly display its skill and beauty in flight. It is from there that the eagle can go to work, spotting prey, raising fledglings, and defending and building its future. An ox, on the other hand, is known to tread the corn and live comfortably in a smaller environment but live highly productive lives where there is order and calmness. So, I must ask, have you answered the location question? Have you found where you come alive?

| | |
|---|---|
| Lion Goal setting and goal-oriented space. | Eagle managerial and structured space that operates from a strong sense of vision. |
| Ox orderly and peaceful space with a clear productive process. | Man, inventive and creative space with a fast pace recovery system. |

# CHAPTER 17

# Curse or Blessing

I would like to draw your attention to the purpose mentioned earlier in the book, which is to bring healing and restoration to the individual.

Blessings and curses exist, and they are a result of dysfunctional humanity, which has its root in one word: sin. The only record we have where these words entered the human ear is from the beginning of the Bible. In this light, we are all broken and living in a broken world.

We are a generation of individuals, most of whom are the same approximate age, having similar ideas, problems, and attitudes. The human suffers from the same generational issues of sin and curse, which are passed down from Adam.

But when God comes into a human life through their faith in Jesus Christ, who is the beginner of a new generation called the blessed (or forgiven) generation, He works to restore the individual to their right status in the spirit, soul, and body. This correction takes place first from within and is the breaking of the curse and the introduction into the blessed life.

The result of this inner work often results in the discovery of your personality type. When an individual access this reality through the help of God, it is as though the scales fall away from their eyes. It is like they hadn't existed before then.

# CHAPTER 18

# Receiving Inner Healing

Most religious experience promises inner peace and healing for its worshipper, and the Christian faith is no different. Because we live in a broken world filled with broken and disenfranchised people, this goal may end up becoming as costly as the worshipper's previous condition.

In my years of counselling, I have come to realize the power of self-discovery in the light of the Gospel. Many may approach this subject from a place of reconciliation, making peace with the offender. This can reach a very deep place to bring about peace, yet it is the inner discovery of one personality and living out of that river that seals the deal. Inner healing stands as a central feature when we deal with the subject of personality types.

After every reconciliation, both parties will still have to live out the rest of their lives in the new light of their past pain, disappointment, and possibly the self-mutilating feeling of regression.

The approach of studying and accepting one personality brings a more powerful awareness of divine reality—a reality that releases the strength of discovery and exploration.

This type of feeling is priceless to the one who finds this power. That is the hope of the Christian worshipper. You want not only religion but the experience of a personal encounter with your creation. As you discover your personality, you will find the essence of life and purpose, your goals for success in life will become attainable.

This is the picture: An individual with the primary personality of Ox has been trying to live as though they had a Lion personality. After years of toiling, they will find themselves broken.

This must be frustrating, knowing that they have become so broken because of the competitive, rigorous, and somewhat harsh lifestyle that litters the life of a broken Lion personality. This Ox personality finally discovers the terrain in which it belongs. Instead of living out the rest of its life to working as a Lion and enduring the brokenness that follows, it discovers there is a better way. A way which comes naturally. This scenario is what unpins the path to inner healing.

This is the eureka moment, when the Ox personality finds and appreciates themself and the beauty of their gifts. They will hit the fields and work with joy. This time, they will give it all they've got without becoming doubtful or fearful.

Each production rate is matchless at this point and their work satisfaction is overwhelming. As the Ox finds its strength from the desire to fill up the barn and to distribute resources, so will other personality types find their most productive instinct and do the same. Its gifts of patience and the power of service consumes every need for pacification and affirmation. Inner healing will become self-generating, and it will begin to flourish.

# CHAPTER 19

# Understanding Role Play in Leadership

When I took the reins of ministering to others in need, I found myself in a place of great perplexity. On one hand, there are people needing direction, healing, and encouragement. On the other hand, here I am, a leader who needs to understand my personality gifts and how to hone my strengths in order to lead most effectively.

It took a while before I could say, "All right, here I am, and this is how I lead." I am so glad this point came so early in the process.

Until this point, you find that you will try and test several leadership styles. So, you may try to lead like an Eagle personality, when you are a Man personality. One of the difficulties is understanding your audience and your message for them.

Effective leadership begins by listening. By listening to the needs of your audience, you can figure out how to communicate the answer to them. The second process is learning. Learning from what has been said. This is the process of taking the needs of your audience into consideration, so that the third and most important process of effective adaptation can begin.

So, if the above module leads to effective communication and leadership, why not ask the leadership question, "What is it that I am hearing and why?" Knowing how you hear will vastly help improve your leadership role. Jesus said take heed how you hear.

The knowledge of your primary personality will enhance how you hear. What you hear could make you an effective leader, since leadership requires effective storytelling and communication. Your personality type will help avoid listening from a place of presumptuousness and impatience.

Another important responsibility as a leader is to bring healing to the broken heart. Empathy plays a major role in moving your audience from a place of despair to a place of hope, where they are ready to win as a team.

Jesus made the privilege of His leadership exclusive when he announced, "The Spirit of the Lord is upon me because he has anointed me to proclaim good news to the poor. He has sent me to proclaim liberty to the captives and recovering of sight to the blind, to set at liberty those who are oppressed" (Luke 4:8).

If your primary personality is an Ox, then you will lean most conversations in the direction of empathy, patience, and hospitality. As one in a leading role, the question to ask is "what do I hear from those I lead?" If I am an Eagle, which is picky about words and prone to fast and swift conclusions, I will surely be willing to demonstrate more empathy than an Ox, which would rather hear the words over and again.

Therefore, the Eagle leader will avoid the temptation to become impatient or—worse—accusatory to the one they lead. The Eagle leader will lead with less presumptuousness because one of their strengths is the ability to visualize the end from the beginning. It is this strength that may become a limiting factor when a broken Eagle is working on team or as a leader in decision-making and execution.

Your success in leadership will largely be determined by your ability to communicate impactfully. Nothing is as powerful as a leader that leads with purpose, as opposed to a leader trying to find the centre of their personality. I experienced this firsthand, because even though I knew my primary personality, I never knew how to appropriate all the passions and drive that came it. So, I almost had to please others or become apologetic in my chosen method and message. This is where many compromises form out of duress. But it is time to locate your core and personality. If you are an Eagle, stay true to soaring in high height. It will take determination and tenacity but only being an Eagle is where you best do leadership, and likewise for the other primary personalities.

# CHAPTER 20

# Developing Leadership Skills

Years ago, I figured out what form of learning had the most impact on my learning process. I realized early what tremendous impact visuals had on me. I can read a book with little retention, but as soon as I see documentary, a live webinar, or a film on the same topic, it will propel me to hunger for more knowledge. It was this realization that gave birth to my insatiable search for wisdom and knowledge.

You cannot develop an Eagle the same way you develop an Ox.

Let me put it this way:

The fledgling needs to develop flight as a major skill. So, by nature, eagles construct their eyries at high elevations—somewhere above two thousand feet. This sends a strong message to the fledglings that flight is their focus. The golden eagle has conquered almost all the northern hemisphere, from the west coast of North America to the east coast of China. They are known for constructing eyries at the cleft of the majestic dolomite mountains, with steep edges that make for a dangerous fall. This environment provides the motivation for the young fledgling's development.

Define your personality type and accept what God has placed in you, so you can align yourself to enjoy the development strategy that will work naturally for you. You can finally accept the pace of your personal development. You will no longer measure your development against others and will defeat self-blame and the temptation to become a copy of others.

The lion and the eagle are both great hunters. One is a master of the air while the other is a master on the land. Yet both have much different development processes. While the eagle will have started honing their hunting skills after only three to six weeks, the cub will be under parental protection for well over a year before doing the same.

The question is, are you an Eagle, a Lion, a Man, or an Ox personality? What methods of development have you mapped out for yourself when reflecting on your primary and secondary personality types?

I must add here that among these personality types, the Man personality tends to lean toward a much slower pace and space of development.

Just as in the natural life circle, humans live under their parental roof until they leave to start their own home, often in their twenties. Recent research shows that because of the economic crises, many young people are returning home to lower overhead costs.

Let us put this mildly: ideal children will be responsible enough to live as successful adults before they venture out. That is long compared to the others in the class of divine personality types.

The inspirational attributes unpinned what the Man personality really is. The natural ability to inspire others makes this personality such an eager leader. They find themselves helping others make their dreams come true, always willing to take the initiative and not afraid to invent or to disrupt. Because of this natural flexibility and the confidence, it displays, the Man personality can lean toward role play instead of exploring their unique role in life. Due to all these distractions, the Man personality may live their entire lives without engaging with the true essence of their personality.

Yet, under most circumstances, the Man personality struggles to find meaning and move forward in life. People connected to this type of personality are often so eager to give support that they miss the often-loud cry for help that is so common with their personality.

# CHAPTER 21

# Leadership Deployment

There is an old saying that goes, "Do not send a boy to do a man's job."

The fact is the cub will someday have to leave its mother's side and fend for itself. The young man needs to leave the comfort of home to venture and start his own family. The eagle will have to jump out of the eyrie into open skies. The calf will eventually be weaned away from the dams (mother) and become a producer to reap the benefit of working.

It is all about the deployment of personality types. At the end of the day, leaders will need to think about replicating the blessings of each. The future depends on raising future leaders that are sound in their personalities.

In general, this concept can become a blueprint that will rescue the next generation. We have been raised in a certain box and thrown into a world that consistently invites us to break boxes and become unique.

They may soon find out that this next generation will not be so willing to leave home. They may not have the courage to face the volatile, uncertain, complex, and ambiguous times. Leadership is knowing when and how to prepare the next generation so they can achieve more than their predecessor.

I break down the wheel of leadership deployment with the acronym LEAD:

Successful deployment begins with effective listening and learning, as we said in the previous chapter. It is only when purpose of learning is comprehended that we can equip future leaders to empower the type of gifting in their community.

Adaptability focuses on pre-deployment, where rooms are created for experimentation. This stage is the costliest stage in leadership deployment, in which leaders may grow discouraged by the uncertainties that this process may bring. Experimentation may send leaders backward in the wheel to further equip or empower the team before deployment can take place.

For a business, this is the time to talk about expanding operations, adding new equipment, or expanding existing facilities. For a church, it is time to start up a satellite church or mission outpost.

I believe it is the dream of any parent or leader to see their children or the ones they lead develop and successfully launch into their recognized place in life. In a cooperative setting, I subscribe to the concept that developing a leader is the main purpose of all leadership. Deployment is the test of leadership. What happens when the leader is not around determines the quality of leadership provided. When a structure is built with deployment as a core value and culture in leadership develop-ment, it naturally creates a healthy room for experimentation, growth, and replication.

Replication is the more positive end of duplication. Duplication is the potential to create an exact copy, while replication is the ability to recreate the same process over many phases. To en-hance your leadership, it is imperative that the four personalities of man are fully understood in order to send the right person out at the right time with the right team.

What is your desired result? As an example, if patience and the long-haul are your attitudinal need, you do not want to involve a Lion or Man personality but a fully matured Eagle or Ox personality.

❧



# CHAPTER 22

# Team Building

John Maxwell once said, "Teamwork makes the dream work."

There is a major blessing to finally having a team that can take you and your organization to another level.

There are people who have successfully built great carriers from the bottom up, helping individuals and companies alike achieve breathtaking goals by simply showing the importance of being on the right team.

These experts will tell you that it takes the right people with the right personalities to set up an unbeatable team. The processes of diversity, inclusion, or programming are not plausible if individuals do not have a real working knowledge of what personality types they possess.

The strength of your team is based on the strength of every individual that makes up the team. The value of your network depends on how good the networks. Therefore, before you join any team or avail your services, you may want to find out if your primary personality can find expression in the group.

I believe this is what employees look for when they interview potential team members. They look for the right fit for their company. If you are going for an interview, my suggestion is to know yourself and be relaxed because those interviewing you may also not have a rounded understanding of the person that they are looking for. Sometimes, all they want is that sweet, fuzzy feeling of "yes!" when you walk into the room.

So, I suggest that you do your due diligence; know the history, the vision, and the core values of the company before your pitch. Ultimately, they need someone, and when you walk in, they will know it from your true mature personality.

If they anticipate a Lion for the job and an Eagle shows up, they will know. I have seen situations where a candidate came in for an interview thoroughly armed with a recently updated resume and every necessary credential, yet the manager decided to go for a complete novice. Yet they found their Eagle.

That story, by the way, was of my wife being employed at a Dutch company while she could not speak or understand Dutch at the time.

What feeling did they get when you walked in? Are they speaking your primary or secondary language? These days, phrases like "creating culture" or "finding your tribe" are often used to describe where people subscribe, belong, fit, or relate.

Whatever context you prefer, just be aware your circle is crucial to development.

Serving a team through your primary personality type creates room of others around you. You need to learn the principle of completing instead of competing. You are no longer threatened by the uniqueness of other divine personalities, but are instead ready to embrace their qualities and collaborate on many levels

So, before you are drafted into a team, ask these questions.

1. What is my primary language?
2. What perspective draws my first responses?
3. How do I hear others?
4. What is my lean in communication?

⚜

CHAPTER 23

# Understanding Team Members

Being a part of something bigger is the bedrock to becoming significant. Many people want to become successful because they feel that it will make them happy, yet it is the feeling of significance that creates happiness.

By impacting the lives of others, you will enjoy the beauty of living. These divine personalities are mankind's service mode. Mostly, we touch people's life when we are patient. Teamwork can go at a pace that is far different from yours.

Your team may be scheduled to complete a project in five months, but it could drag on for a year or two. The question is, how much patience will you allow, and will you keep the right attitude in the process? How will you bring understanding to the team? The greater the accomplishment of a team, the deeper the understanding of everyone on the team ought to be.

We learn to honour everyone on the team simply by knowing their personality type. It is very seldom you dishonour those you are willing to serve respectfully. On a team, you will learn to celebrate the strength of fellow team members. You will be able to identify certain personality types that need your help and attention in certain aspects of their lives.

✣

CHAPTER 24

# Romantic Relationships

"You need to marry to enjoy it, not endure it."

Relationships have been the cause of brokenness more than any other institution on Earth, by far. At the core of any relationship is the deep feeling of love and being loved. Love is that stimulus that encourages humanity, whether rich or poor, to enter union with each other.

Relationships, in general, begin with a dream of growing together, working together, and building a life together. The Bible even endorsed this with many quotes. One of them says, "Find a good spouse, you find a good life, and even more: the favour of God" (Proverbs 18:22).

The health of all relationships is hinged on how much each person knows about themselves. I often counsel couples before marriage, and in one of those sessions, I would ask a question like "how did you arrive at this point, knowing he or she is the right one?" They usually begin by politely describing all the good aspects that have informed their decision.

The answers would be followed by a nice list of requests for the other person. They would describe beautiful deeds that, if continued, would give more meaning to their relationship.

We often think that if the other person acts right, we will do right. That's a reverse in relationships. When you find someone who is interested in you, and there is a spark of excitement brewing, you know what I mean?

Ask yourself how you can make a difference in this person's life. Then ask, "If this person falls head over heel for me, do I have what it takes to sustain a healthy relationship for this person's spirit, soul, and body?" Thirdly, ask how you can best facilitate this person's growth. And fourthly, ask if you can protect them spiritually, emotionally, and financially.

Knowing human nature and how self-centred we are, by now, many would have said, "I have a lot of love to give so, I think I can."

So, let us take an examination. If you are a Lion and you are not aware that the primary personality of your partner is an Ox, how can you appropriately love them? How can you show your love as a doer and a driver to one that is stable, satisfied, and content without your irritations concerning pace and achievements getting in the way?

These are overly complex issues if you don't do loving research like the one you are doing now by reading this book. I am not saying it is impossible to do so. Being married for a couple of years now, with many ups and downs, I've learned how important it is to deposit understanding and knowledge into your emotional and spiritual bank.

There is a statement that goes, "You need to marry to enjoy it, not endure it." Love motivates many to endure their marriages, but a robust understanding of who we are and what we carry into a relationship is what will determine how much you enjoy it.

Before you say, "I do," do you know your spiritual profile? Have you done your spiritual due diligence to know what your personality types are and if they work well together?

You see, many may have an idea of who they need to have for a partner. For example, a Lion (driven and persistent) may end up with an Eagle (the complex and sensitive) while a Man (the inspirer) may end up with an Ox (the stable and satisfied). This may result in regular conflict, negative verbal exchanges, or worse, the silent treatment. Rather than the complexity of consistent disagreement and reconciliation, a good understanding of your spiritual profiling will such ensure mutual respect for each other's strengths and weaknesses.

Individuals who desire a personality must first ask themselves who they are and if they understand the negatives and positives of such. This awareness is so worth it. It helps to harness the empathy and preparedness needed for daily adjustment in areas of communication and financial intelligence, building healthy emotional support systems around your spouse and children.

It is wise not to presume that love is all it takes to be happy in a relationship. Sure, you need love as a solid foundation. But as they said, assumption is the mother of mess-ups. It is far better to know who you are, your character, your identity, and what makes you who you need to become for your spouse.

# CHAPTER 25

# Personality Adoption

There are cases I like to call "personality adoption." These are situations where individuals will adopt a preferred personality simply because they enjoy being seen and respected in that way. As such, they blend into that environment very well at the time. Because people generally gravitate toward outward displays of strength, confidence, and charisma, we find many adopt such personalities, when on the inside, they are much different.

By declaring themselves a Lion when their primary personality is an Ox, they suppress the warm and lovely traits of the Ox. If such an individual attracts an Ox, they may become resentful or regretful because God is supposedly reflecting some of their weaknesses. Usually, this should serve as a place to draw healing and restoration, but in the case of personality adoption, this individual will be seriously deterred from such a process.

Often, we hear that opposites attracts. That may be the case, but goes unsaid is that as individuals, we have opposing sides in our personal lives as well. You have a positive and a negative side. Even if you feel the other person is your opposite, it doesn't mean they are, as many experiences show. You may not have yet discovered the full range of qualities your personality type possesses. So, this person has come into your life to shine a light on areas that were either closed to you or that you did not want to reveal.

Usually, as God will have it, it could be to present an opportunity that would bring awareness to your assumed negative side. If accepted, this would, in turn, be the source of restoration and healing for you.

Every romantic relationship based on healthy love is presented with an opportunity for healing and restoration. It is interesting how we feel hurt when the ones closest to us try to interfere with our weak side, yet we allow others to help fix us from afar—go figure!

This statement "opposites attract" can raise either negative or positive interactions based on our understanding of spiritual profiling. They can bring up complexity, which sometimes leads to divorce. We grapple more with trying to fix what's negative about our spouses when relationships are actually about the understanding of personality as a gift from God. "Opposites attract" is a phrase and not a rule. Spouses may not be comfortable with their weaknesses being reflected.

This is one of the reasons why you need to understand your personality type and your spiritual profile. Also, know and embrace both your strengths and your weaknesses. Be open to making it a priority and create strategies for growth within your relationship. Reach out to God for healing and accept help from your spouse or future spouse.

At this point, you may wonder, "Can my spouse understand this?" If you apply what you learn, your spouse will begin to feel your effort. They will respect the space you create for growth and appreciate you even more. This success will create the same feeling of achievement in your hearts.

So, going forward, it's good to ask these questions:

- What is my primary personality type?
- What is my secondary personality type?
- What primary and secondary type can I best serve?
- Which personality type works well with my healing process?
- How can I connect to such help?

How Restoration Look Like

CHAPTER 26

# Table of strengths and weaknesses

| FACE OF A LION – STRENGTH | |
| --- | --- |
| • Strong willed | • Tenacious |
| • Competitive | • Good organizers |
| • Not easily discouraged | • Ambitious |
| • Get things done | • Purposeful |
| • Sure | • Courageous |
| • Forceful | • Takes Charge |
| • Daring | • Loves conflict |
| • Decisive | • Sees the big picture |
| • Mover | • Adventurous |
| • Loves a challenge. | • Quick thinkers |
| • Productive | • Leaders |
| • Bold | • Admired |
| • Outspoken | • Assertive |
| • Unconquerable | • Pioneering |
| • Loves pressure | • Loudly Intense |
| • Loves correcting | • Practical |
| • Loves productive situations | • Efficient |
| • Aggressive | • Determined |
| • Goal-oriented | • Persistent |
| • Independent | • Strong and Brave |
| • Confrontational | • Objective |
| • Dominant | • Not shaking |
| • Never wastes time | • Directly spoken |
| • Direct | |

| FACE OF A MAN – STRENGTH | |
| --- | --- |
| • Popular | • Adventurous |
| • Charming | • Admirable |
| • Open-minded | • Quick thinkers |
| • Life of the party | • Leaders |
| • Loves a crowd | • Assertive |
| • Wonderful humour | • Pioneering |
| • Joyful | • Light-hearted |
| • Loud | • Accepting |
| • Funny | • Trusting |
| • Representative | • Generous |
| • Helpful | • Appreciative |
| • Hopeful | • Sensitive |
| • Caring | • Empathetic |
| • Persuasive | • Bold |
| • Inspiring | • Boisterous |
| • Animated | • Sociable |
| • Refreshing | • Expressive |
| • Encourages others | • Verbal |
| • Highly discerning | • Hospitable |
| • Higher energy | • Adaptive |
| • Physical touching | • Promotional |
| • Great storytellers | • Spontaneous |
| • Great in mediation | |
| • Great visionary (Sees the big picture) | |

| FACE OF AN OX – STRENGTH | |
|---|---|
| • Good Natured | • Supportive |
| • Analysers for the love knowledge | • Kind |
| • Analysers for the fun of it | • Neighbourly |
| • Loyal | • Deep friendship |
| • Soft Spoken | • Low key |
| • Obedient | • Detailed |
| • Light-hearted | • List maker |
| • Accepting | • Accurate |
| • Trusting | • Conscious |
| • Generous | • Reserved |
| • Appreciative | • Reliable |
| • Stable | • Resilient |
| • Objective | • Understanding |
| • Decisive | • Endurance Long |
| • Structured | hauled mentality |
| • Hospitable | • Super empathetic |
| • Pleasant | • Great team member |
| • Willing | • Generational thinkers |
| • Agreeable | • Great Parenting disposition |

| FACE OF AN EAGLE – STRENGTH | |
| --- | --- |
| • Careful | • Reflective |
| • Complex | • Analyse to improve self |
| • Self-Sacrificing | • Friendly loyal to a few. |
| • High Standards | • Soft spoken |
| • Respectful | • Obedient |
| • Scheduled | • Quietly Intense |
| • Orderly | • Practical |
| • Deep Thinker | • Efficient |
| • Planner | • Persistent |
| • Intense Listener | • Sensitive |
| • Idealist | Feel things deeply |
| • Thoughtful | • Skilled |
| • God fearing | • Competent |
| • Precise | • Alert |
| • Finishes the Job | • Zealous |
| • Desirous to give themselves | • Servants |
| • Devout | • Detailed |
| • Loves fine art | • Loyal (Very deep friend and very few) |
| • Great concentration | |
| • Time-conscious | • Professional approach |
| • Protective | |

| WEAKNESS IN THE PERSONALITY TYPES |
| --- |

**LION – Weaknesses**
- Controlling
- Domineering
- Presumptuous
- Anger issues
- Workaholics
- Always in the right
- Retaliatory

**FACE OF THE MAN - Weakness**
- Distracted
- Discontinuity
- Bitterness
- Outburst of anger
- Casting blames
- Lying or exaggerating
- Loners

**FACE OF THE OX – Weaknesses**
- Slothfulness
- Time wasting
- Evasiveness
- Susceptible to abusive relationship
- Substance abuse
- Tirelessly idealist
- A lack of practicality

**FACE OF THE EAGLE – Weakness**
- Critical attitude
- Very stubborn
- Hold grudges for long period of times (sometimes unforgiving)
- Insecurity
- Defensive
- Self-pity
- Loneliness

$\infty$



# CHAPTER 27

# Restoration Project

*Overview of How to Restore Personality*

"As for the likeness of their faces, they four had the face of a man, and the face of a Lion, on the right side: and they four had the face of an Ox on the left side; they four also had the face of an Eagle" (Ezekiel 1:10).

(For further research on the four personalities, read Ezekiel 10:4 and Revelation 4:7)

Although this is not a comprehensive overview, the hope is that it provides a framework for you to build on. I trust it will help you map out your personal restoration process, and going forward, you can help others with theirs. It can also be valuable for group-life classes to help others find healing and restoration.

When you talk of healing and restoration, talk about a person who has finally found purpose and is able to flow with it. The first line of thought should be that nothing is worth it unless it feeds purpose. The urgency to change the world or make a difference in peoples' lives will overwhelm the fear and doubt.

Imagine a Lion that never got the right training to reach restoration. They will only use their assertiveness to control and boss everyone around, usually due to their heighted sense of sarcasm, and will create more broken people around them. An Eagle will become even more critical and lash out with negative comments, tearing into others with vicious claw of passive aggression. An Ox personality may go the route of slothfulness and becomes careless about life, which often leads to addictive practices and behaviours. They will succumb to abuse of all kinds due to a broken identity, and the face of Man will end up a very bitter individual, relentless in condemning, accusing, and retaliating against others.

The Lion personality is the doer's personality. Doer simply means the Lion is that individual that seems to have a driven approach to life. He or she has this attitude of "if it must be done, it should be done now." They are the persistent ones. They will find way to bring results, the obstacle notwithstanding. Jesus called himself the Lion of the tribe of Judah.

A restored Lion becomes a gentle yet confident personality who uses their persistence and goal-oriented determination to protect the timid and fearful. They will be challenged out of selflessness and will become tireless in their drive to see to the wellbeing of all. The competitive edge is used for a more constructive purpose as a motivator, coach, or a mentor to blaze the trail for others and set a great example of a humble achiever.

The Man personality is the inspirational personality. They live to bring joy to the lives of others. They are highly motivated to see others reach their goals and are satisfied only when others have discovered their assignment. These are the pure people-persons. They thrive in an environment where others are being empowered, and they will do their part in the empowerment process with great delight. They are your original motivators, coaches, and instructors. One outstanding quality of the Man personality is the ability to kick off any major project. They love brainstorm sessions and the creative process.

The restored Man personality is an inspirer that has destroyed that nagging feeling of performance and people pleasing. They will no longer try to impress everyone and be everyone else's helper for fear of not being accepted. The Man will be an inspirer that surrenders to the fact that inspiration is subjective—it all depends on people's willingness to receive and adapt ideas. They will use innovation and creativity as a place of peace and joy to inspire others to dream the impossible. They will understand that the power of stepping back sometimes means going forward and being led is not a loss of influence.

The Ox is that personality that appears satisfied with life. This satisfaction come from a deep place of divine assurance and peace. They are very satisfied with whatever they have achieved, small or large. They have an inbuilt strength of solid contentment and they have no pressing desire to destroy the peace for anything. They are the patient and understanding ones that act as a haven for others in trouble. They are your first-class hosts or hostesses with a tireless desire to see people come to their place of rest. They are big in the hospitality and care business and have the strong capacity to create stable wealth for the next generation through patient enterprise. They are your angel-like individual with a disposition of peace for the world.

The Ox personality is restored to confidence and self-worth. It is a place of value and responsibility. They have been restored to the idea that they are needed more than they realize. So, re-alization and self-awareness are the miracles in the restoration process of the Ox personality. The restored Ox personality will be very evident in their level of productivity. In all these per-sonality types, the Ox leans toward really making it to financial fulfillment. The restored Ox will be delivered from the place of complacency in self-development; they will begin to appreciate and celebrate their personal achievement.

The Eagle personality is the ultimate divine representative for a perfect vision. They are the individuals with a strong deter-mination for the future and almost futuristic in disposition. They are, in many respects, the most disciplined among the other personality. They are the highest achievers, with a strong taste for winners in any field they choose. This is because of their no-nonsense approach to life. When in enterprise, they are truly the divine standard for excellence. Due to their precision thinking, they are mostly decisive individuals with little room for distraction. Safe to say, they love figures due to the solid conclusions those bring. For the Eagle, there is no room for error, showing God's divine gifts of knowledge, wisdom, and power. Hence the original Eagle personality is great in trade as the data industries, architectural industries, IT specialists, surgical doctors, and other industries that require precision.

The restored Eagle finds rest in simple things. Restoration of the Eagle includes the acceptance of others and their various challenges. Eagles will become less critical of themselves and will begin to see failure as part of the growth process, opening to experimentation and disruptions. Restored Eagles will accept their wrongdoing and make amends. The restored Eagle is a powerful visionary that will become open to sharing and leadership, instead of the assumption that they will be misunderstood. The Eagle personality suffers from the weakness of assumption. It can be a real struggle because of the deep feeling that no one can meet their standards. This mindset may have been the cause that stimulated the loner instinct in the Eagle. It creates an invisible barrier that screens out worthwhile advice, but restoration helps the Eagle to let their guard down for life improvement and growth.

⚘



**"I** will praise thee; for I am fearfully and wonderfully made marvellous are thy works; and that my soul knoweth right well" (Psalm 139:14).

This verse firmly speaks about the mystery of God's wisdom, as to the marvellous combination of such powerful personalities to create one integral being called mankind. Intricately interwoven, these personality types are a worthy study.

In retrospect, we must develop a great working relationship with God and ourselves before any other relationships such as people, money, career, and even having children, so as not to become so engrossed in others that we neglect the riches and the glory of God.

| Left | Right |
| --- | --- |
| Face of Man (The Leader)<br><br>• Inspirer<br><br>• Enthusiast<br><br>• Great starter | Face of Ox (The Follower)<br><br>• The Satisfied<br><br>• The Content<br><br>• The Gentle (Angel like) |
| Face Lion (The Leader)<br><br>• The Doer<br><br>• The Driver<br><br>• The Persistent | Face of Eagles (The Follower)<br><br>• Complex<br><br>• Cautious<br><br>• Sensitive |

Books By
ALEXANDER O. EMOGHENE

Alexander O. Emoghene
HAMBRE
DE
IMPACTO
...algo está a punto
de cambiar

websites: **www.tulippublications.com**

Follow us on: **facebook.com/tulipseminars**

www.ingramcontent.com/pod-product-compliance
Lightning Source LLC
LaVergne TN
LVHW091402210726
843527LV00020B/402/J